Belair Early Years Writing

Jean Evans

Acknowledgements

The author and publishers would like to thank the staff and children of Rainbow Nursery, Durham High School; Durham Chorister School; The Childcare Centre, Darlington College of Technology and St Oswald's Pre-school Learning Centre, Newton Aycliffe, for their invaluable help in the production of displays for this book. The author would also like to add a special thank you to her daughter Charlotte, George Dent Nursery School and Great Aycliffe Town Council Pre-school Learning Centres, for additional help with the activities.

Under the Sea (page 16)

Published by Collins, An imprint of HarperCollins*Publishers*
77 – 85 Fulham Palace Road, Hammersmith, London, W6 8JB

Browse the complete Collins catalogue at
www.collinseducation.com

© HarperCollins*Publishers* Limited 2012
Previously published in 2007 by Folens
First published in 2004 by Belair Publications

10 9 8 7 6 5 4 3 2 1

ISBN-13 978-0-00-744801-2

Jean Evans asserts her moral rights to be identified as the author of this work

British Library Cataloguing in Publication Data
A Catalogue record for this publication is available from the British Library

All Early learning goals, Areas of learning and development, and Aspects of learning quoted in this book are taken from the *Statutory Framework for the Early Years Foundation Stage*, Department for Education, 2012 (available at www.education.gov.uk/publications). This information is licensed under the terms of the Open Government Licence (www.nationalarchives.gov.uk/doc/open-government-licence).

Every effort has been made to trace copyright holders and to obtain their permission for the use of copyright material. The authors and publishers will gladly receive any information enabling them to rectify any error or omission in subsequent editions.

Cover concept: Mount Deluxe   Cover design: Linda Miles, Lodestone Publishing
Cover photography: Nigel Meager   Commissioning editor: Zöe Nichols
Editor: Nancy Candlin   Page layout: Philippa Jarvis
Illustrations: Jane Conway   Photography: Roger Brown and Kelvin Freeman

p16 *Sea Nettle*, NHPA © Tom and Therisa Stack; p28 *Children in Library* © Angela Hempton Family Life Picture Library; p32 *Children in Restaurant* © Pizza Express; p52 *Harry and the Robots* (published by Gullane Children's Books), reprinted by permission of the author.

Printed and bound by Printing Express Limited, Hong Kong

MIX
Paper from responsible sources
FSC® C007454

Contents

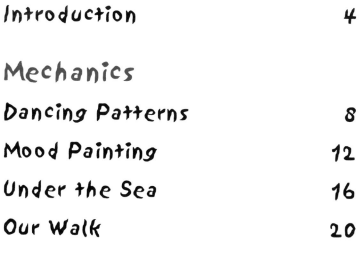

Introduction

The **Belair Early Years** series has been well-loved by early years educators working with the under-fives for many years. This re-launched edition of these practical resource books offers popular, tried and tested ideas, all written by professionals working in early years education. The inspirational ideas will support educators in delivering the three characteristics of effective teaching and learning identified in the Statutory Framework for the Early Years Foundation Stage 2012: playing and exploring, active learning, and creating and thinking critically.

The guiding principles at the heart of the EYFS Framework 2012 emphasise the importance of the unique child, the impact of positive relationships and enabling environments on children's learning and development, and that children develop and learn in different ways and at different rates. The 'hands on' activities in **Belair Early Years** fit this ethos perfectly and are ideal for developing the EYFS prime areas of learning (Communication and language, Physical development, Personal, social and emotional development) and specific areas of learning (Literacy, Mathematics, Understanding the world, Expressive arts and design) which should be implemented through a mix of child-initiated and adult-led activities. Purposeful play is vital for children's development, whether leading their own play or participating in play guided by adults. Where appropriate, suggestions for Free Play opportunities are identified.

Throughout this book full-colour photography is used to offer inspiration for presenting and developing children's individual work with creative display ideas for each theme. Display is highly beneficial as a stimulus for further exploration, as well as providing a visual communication of ideas and a creative record of children's learning journeys. In addition to descriptions of the activities, each theme in this book provides clear Learning Intentions and extension ideas and activities as Home Links to involve parents/carers in their child's learning.

This title, **Writing**, particularly supports children's progress towards attaining the Early Learning Goals in the Literacy and Expressive arts and design areas of learning. Children often employ writing for a purpose naturally as they play, for example, writing shopping lists or making birthday cards. Exploring a range of creative media helps children to express ideas. Often writing becomes an integral part of this expression with the labels and captions they write to identify and describe their work.

Emergent writing can be encouraged by :
- ensuring that writing materials are available in different classroom areas, including outdoors, for example role-play and scientific investigation
- providing opportunities for children to develop control over large arm as well as finer finger movements
- providing a print rich environment and drawing attention to print in the locality
- modelling writing for a purpose, for example, writing a 'thank you' card together
- planning activities to develop phonic awareness
- acting as scribe if necessary to support a child's early attempts to express ideas.

With the above encouragement, children will learn to:
- understand the role of print and writing as a means of communication
- develop the required motor skills for writing
- begin to recognise letters by sound as well as shape
- confidently attempt some letters and make phonetically plausible attempts at words before asking for help if necessary
- use writing to identify and describe their work
- use writing to express ideas, both factual and creative.

Always praise children positively for writing attempts so that they develop a confident and enthusiastic approach to this essential means of communication.

I hope that adults and children alike will enjoy exploring the activities in this book.

Jean Evans

The book is subdivided into four chapters, each one associated with a specific aspect of the development of early writing skills. These are then subdivided into individual display themes, chosen to capture the interest of young children.

Mechanics

This introductory theme emphasises the need to develop children's control over large movements with exciting physical activities, before progressing to the finer movement skills needed for writing.

Writing for a Purpose

Children then move on from large-scale physical activities to writing and making marks for a variety of purposes, such as using creative materials to represent their ideas, designing recipes and menus, writing letters and making birthday cards.

Names, Labels and Captions

As children's skills develop they are encouraged to write their names to record preferences, feel letters of the alphabet, read name labels and write labels of their own.

Letters and Words

Finally, children progress to reading and writing simple words. As they begin to discover links between reading and writing, they are invited to create a display about a favourite author.

Within the main themes, each individual display theme includes specific learning intentions related to emergent writing. There are also helpful starting points to enable practitioners to include preparation of the display and organisation of the accompanying activities into their planning. In addition, ideas are given to promote learning areas across the curriculum, under the headings 'Language and Literacy', 'Mathematics', 'Creative Work' and investigation into 'Our World'. Included in these ideas are opportunities to develop physical skills and enhance personal, social and emotional development.

Children learn a great deal through their own explorations as they play and a section on 'Free Play' within each individual theme demonstrates how to provide such valuable opportunities. It is important to include the outdoor environment when providing children with opportunities to explore writing. For this reason, all individual themes include related suggestions for outdoor activities. Parents and carers play a significant part in a child's education. With this in mind, individual themes include suggestions, or 'Home Links', for extending ideas and activities into the home environment. Parents and carers should always be encouraged to share their expertise, take an active part in activities and help to provide resources.

Writing in Play Areas

It is important to remember that writing can take place in all play areas, including outdoors. Children should be able to explore freely and make their own discoveries when they visit play areas, with and without adult support.

Role-play

Many of the resources suggested for setting up the graphics area could be used to extend opportunities for writing during role-play. Having a postbox as a permanent feature away from the area will encourage children to write letters during role-play and post them.

Outdoors

● Supply a box of mark-making resources so that children can create labels, such as car number plates. Also have ready a good supply of clipboards and writing materials.

Creative Play

● Encourage children to use just their fingers and hands to make marks in materials with different textures such as sand, shaving foam, cornflour and water, clay and dough before introducing tools such as small twigs and combs.

● Provide opportunities for children to make marks with paint using everyday objects such as feathers, sponges, toothbrushes and cotton buds.

● Invite children to write about how they make their models by drawing pictures or writing words about the items they have used.

Construction and Small World Play

● Display maps of the locality and photographs of buildings to inspire children's ideas. Supply them with clipboards and writing materials so that they can draw plans and record their actions. Also encourage children to write captions and signs to enhance play with small world characters.

Investigation

● Always include writing tools and materials during adult-led investigations so that children can record the results of their observations. Leave clipboards alongside interest tables for children to record their ideas and observations.

Setting up a Graphics Area

In addition to providing writing opportunities throughout the early years environment, every setting should have an area where children can explore a range of mark-making tools and materials.

Positioning and Defining the Area

- Position the area where there is good natural light. If possible, enclose it on three sides to give children a feeling of privacy and to encourage concentration. Attach appropriate pictures, posters and photographs to screens and walls, and include examples of writing by both adults and children, ensuring that different scripts are represented.

Storage and Management of Equipment

- When setting up a storage system in your graphics area, it is important to make all items easily accessible to the children. They should be able to find what they want and know exactly where to put that item after they have finished. Screens with shelves can be used to store some items, for example paper of different sizes and tubs of crayons, felt-tip pens and pencils. Create shadows by drawing round the base of the storage containers on sticky-backed plastic and attach these to the shelves. Smaller resources, such as paperclips and sticky tape, can be stored in plastic containers. Label all containers clearly to indicate the contents and arrange them on a table or shelf. Provide low display boards so that children can display their work themselves.

The Role of the Adult

- Be a good role model. Demonstrate how writing is a means of communication, for example by compiling lists, filling in the register, creating labels and writing letters in front of the children.

- Always encourage the children to see themselves as writers. Give lots of praise to build up their self-confidence.

- Share experiences of writing with the children, for example by scribing a child's story alongside his/her picture, or by writing an invitation to a visitor and asking the children to write their names on it.

- Be ready to answer questions related to writing, such as "What does this say?" or "Will you show me how to write 'Daddy'?"

- Help the children to make links between print and the spoken word and refer to letters by their names and sounds.

- Include children's writing and drawings in displays and provide opportunities for them to notice print all around them, from the large and attractive notice board in your entrance hall to small signs about hand washing in the cloakroom areas.

- Make sure that children are able to observe writing in books, magazines and leaflets throughout your setting.

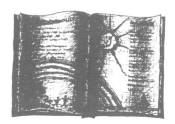

Dancing Patterns

Learning Intentions

- To engage in activities requiring large circular and linear movements.

- To use clockwise and anticlockwise movements.

Starting Points

- Have some fun sessions waving flags and streamers. Make the streamers from long strips of brightly-coloured tissue, and flags from squares of thick paper that have been coloured by the children. Tape individual streamers and flags to lengths of dowelling. Glue small pieces of sponge over the ends of the dowelling to avoid accidents when children are waving them.

- Talk about the children's experience of flags. Have they ever seen one fluttering on the top of a flagpole? Make large flags from cotton sheeting. Invite the children to hold the flags they have made and try to 'flap' them like the wind.

- Play 'train' games with one child acting as guard, raising and lowering a red or green flag to signal to a 'train' of children to start or stop.

- Pass around the streamers and talk about who might use them, for example cheerleaders or people at a carnival or in a procession. Try waving the streamers around in big circles at first and then in circles of different sizes. Encourage the children to change from one movement to another by calling out "Up and down" and "Round and round".

Follow the lines

line patterns

up and down

streamers

The children made linear and circular patterns with the streamers and flags.

side to side

The children painted circles and lines with thick and thin brushes.

circle patterns

flags

round and round

Display

● Prepare the backing for a display using brightly-coloured frieze paper. Invite the children to help you to cut out some spirals from coloured card and use these as a border on the display.

● Talk about the movements the children made when they were waving the flags and streamers. Provide large pieces of paper and thick brushes and invite them to paint lines and circles using these same movements. Cut around the children's paintings, creating circles with those that were painted with a circular movement and rectangles from those that have lines on them. Mount the paintings on contrasting paper and attach to the backing paper. Add a caption and labels.

Free Play

● Set up a table below the display covered in a brightly-coloured cloth and arrange some ribbons, maracas, streamers and flags on it. Stand a full-length safety mirror alongside so that children can watch themselves as they wave the objects from the table.

● Stand a box of streamers on a clear floor space alongside a tape recorder with dance music. Encourage the children to play the music themselves and to wave the streamers in circles in time to it.

Language and Literacy

● Look at letter sounds that can be written using just circular movements, such as 'o', 'c' and 's', and ask the children to draw them in the air with a finger. Then ask them to try to 'draw' them by waving a flag. Repeat with letters formed from straight lines such as 'l' and 'z'.

● Make a 'sound box' covered in colourful paper with a hole in the lid. Post some large cards into it depicting the letters used in the above activity. Invite the children to take turns to pull out a card, draw it in the air with a streamer, say the sound and then post it back in the box.

● Leave plentiful supplies of large paper, pens and pencils alongside the display to encourage children to draw the patterns they have made with the streamers and flags.

Mathematics

● Provide each child with a flag or streamer and use positional language to instruct them, for example "Wave your flag up and down beside the window" or "Wave your streamer in a circle next to the sand tray".

● Develop counting skills by asking children to copy your movements, for example wave a flag up and down three times, counting aloud.

● Explore pattern by asking the children to paint parallel lines along the back of a long strip of wallpaper using a small paint roller, and then to add straight lines at regular intervals to create a railway track. Provide toy trains for free play on the track.

● Have fun playing ring games, running round hoops and drawing chalk circles to raise awareness of circular patterns.

● Walk along planks, hop along straight chalk lines and ride cars along straight tracks to raise awareness of straight lines.

Creative Work

- Tape a large piece of paper to the underside of a table and provide a blanket on the floor for children to lie on. Invite them to lie on their backs and draw patterns on the paper under the table using felt-tip pens.

- Play marching music and parade around the room waving flags.

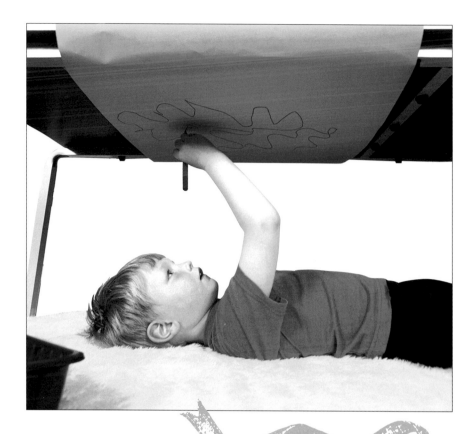

Our World

- Suggest that children pretend to be painters, painting fences, gates and walls with large decorators' brushes and water. Create patterns outside on the floor with smaller brushes.

- Leave a box of flags and streamers outdoors so that children can wave them in the wind.

Home Links

- Explain to parents or carers the importance of encouraging children to develop stronger arm and hand muscles before expecting them to write recognisable letters, and supply them with a sheet of suitable activities, for example, throwing and catching balls, waving ribbons or kneading dough.

- Send home a flag and streamer with each child along with a sheet of games for parents and children to play together.

Mood Painting

Learning Intentions

- To manipulate objects with increasing control.

- To hold mark-making tools correctly.

Starting Points

- Invite the children to sit or lie comfortably on floor cushions whilst they listen to relaxing pieces of recorded music such as Debussy's *Clair de Lune* or Bach's *Air on a G String*. Talk about how the music makes the children feel and encourage them to express their feelings using appropriate vocabulary such as 'dreamy', 'sleepy' or 'happy'.

- Play some contrasting music such as Rimsky Korsakov's *Flight of the Bumble Bee* or Tchaikovsky's *1812 Overture*. How does this music make the children feel? Support them in finding the words to express their emotions.

- Play some 'angry' music such as *The Storm Movement* from Beethoven's *Pastoral Symphony* and invite the children to invent an angry dance to accompany it.

- Promote a feeling of calm at the end of the activity by listening once more to some relaxing music.

While listening to different types of music, the children painted pictures to reflect their moods.

Mood Paintings

Display

- Back the display board with a brightly-coloured paper. Draw different facial expressions on teddy bear faces and add them to the display.

- Set up an 'artists' area' with a choice of easels and tables. Supply a good range of paints, brushes and paper of contrasting colours and sizes. Talk to the children about their earlier experiences of listening to music. Can they remember how they felt? Which music did they enjoy most? Can they say why? Did any of the pieces make them feel unhappy, angry or excited? Invite the children to take turns to choose the music to play and encourage them to paint freely as they listen. Allow the paintings to dry and mount them in a contrasting colour. Attach them to the background paper on the display board.

- Ask the children to think of words to describe how they felt as they were painting. Print these words in large, clear lettering and attach them to the display along with a suitable caption to explain the activity.

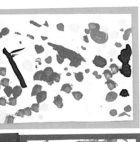

Free Play

- Set up a tape recorder and mark-making equipment on a table so that children can draw pictures whilst they listen to music of their choice. Label the tapes clearly with words and drawings so that the children can identify the type of music, for example a sleeping face for dreamy music, a sad face for mournful music and a smiling face for cheerful, rousing music.

- Hang pictures of faces displaying different emotions in the mark-making and creative areas to stimulate children's ideas as they paint and draw freely.

Language and Literacy

- Make a face-shaped 'feelings' book and invite the children to draw different facial expressions on each page. Scribe captions for the children as they talk to you about their drawings.

- Sing the traditional song *If You're Happy and You Know It* and invite the children to make up verses relating to feeling happy.

Mathematics

Our faces show our feelings

- Play music with a regular beat, such as military band marching music, and suggest the children make marks on a long strip of paper in time to the beat. Have they created a regular pattern?

- Prompt the children to count beats as you play a percussion instrument, and then ask them to tap the same number of beats on an instrument of their choice.

Creative Work

- Encourage the children to express their emotions by moving freely to contrasting pieces of music.

- Examine a collection of musical instruments. Talk about the different sounds and effects that can be created.

- Make musical instruments such as shakers and drums from recycled materials and use them to accompany recorded music.

- Invite a musician or older child to talk about and play an instrument as the children listen.

Home Links

- Explain to parents and carers how children have been talking about their emotions and then painting and drawing them. Encourage the adults to talk with their children about contrasting emotional experiences at home, such as visiting the dentist or enjoying a fairground ride, and to draw pictures of the events.

Our World

- Take the children for a walk on a windy day and pause to talk about how they feel as the wind blows around their faces and bodies. Encourage them to draw and paint pictures of the experience on their return.

- Run around outside during a shower and encourage the children to experience how the raindrops feel on their upturned faces and hands. Afterwards, ask them to draw what they think their faces looked like as they took part in the experience. Were they happy, worried, excited or uncomfortable?

Under the Sea

Learning Intentions

- To engage in activities requiring hand-eye coordination.

- To draw lines and circles.

Starting Points

- Visit the library with a group of children to borrow books about life under the sea. Look at the books together and talk about the different creatures that live there.

- Look at the books or posters of sea creatures and draw children's attention to the shapes and patterns; for example, circular jellyfish with long curly tentacles and the patterns of scales on the surface of a fish.

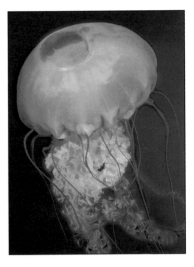

Display

- Join two large pieces of blue frieze paper together to form a sheet large enough to cover the display board. Spread this on the floor and invite the children to paint it to represent waves using different techniques such as printing wavy lines with sponges and rollers. Talk about the range of colours they might use. Allow the paper to dry and attach it to the display board.

16

- Create a border by attaching thin strips of green tissue and Cellophane around the top and sides of the display to create the effect of dangling seaweed. Glue a layer of sandpaper to the base of the display.

- Make a treasure chest from a recycled box and fill it with foil coins and coloured Cellophane jewels. Attach it to the sandpaper at the bottom of the display.

- Stick the children's sea creatures (see 'Creative Work') to the background and entitle the display 'Under the Sea', written in clear lettering on an eel-shaped length of paper.

Free Play

- Set up an exploration table below the wall display where children can trace patterns with fingers and sticks in a shallow tray of dry sand and then copy them using a selection of paper and writing equipment.

- Supply sticks and clay tools to press patterns into dough and clay.

- Spread shaving foam or thick paint over a washable surface. Provide children with a selection of strong cardboard strips with notches cut at intervals so that they can create wavy patterns.

Language and Literacy

- Create a game board by backing a large sheet of card with 'under the sea' themed wrapping paper. Stick three white squares down each side and six blue 'pool' shapes down the centre. Make some square picture cards depicting the displayed sea creatures. Print out the initial letters of the creatures, cut around them and stick one in each 'pool'. Join the squares to the 'pools' with ribbon. Invite the children to choose a picture card, or plastic sea creature, find the initial letter in one of the 'pools', and then follow the ribbon to decide on which square to put the card or creature.

- Write labels depicting the names of the creatures on the main display and attach them alongside each one. Make a spare set of cards and invite the children to match the words to those on the display.

- Play 'I Spy' relating to the creatures on the display.

Mathematics

- Use textured materials to create 'feely' tiles such as sandpaper zigzags and sponge circles glued to the surface of thick card. Invite the children to feel the patterns with their fingers.

- Use wood offcuts to make shape-printing blocks by gluing on circles, squares, rectangles and triangles created from curls of string or sponge. Demonstrate how to dip the block into thick paint and print repeat patterns along a strip of card.

- Draw straight lines and circles on the ground and play games involving balancing along the lines and jumping in and out of the circles. Provide the children with chalk to draw their own lines and circles.

Creative Work

● Create brightly-coloured fish shapes from fluorescent paper. Invite the children to draw zigzag, circular or wavy lines on small triangles of fluorescent paper, and then glue them to make a fish shape.

● Ask the children to look at pictures of the patterns on jellyfish. Cut jellyfish shapes from card and suggest that they draw straight lines radiating down the jellyfish using a thick black crayon. Cover the card with bubble wrap so that the lines show through and attach strands of wool to form tentacles.

● Draw other sea creatures on card, as suggested by the children using books for ideas. Invite them to cut them out and draw appropriate patterns on the surface of each one.

Our World

● Visit a fishmonger or fish stall in a market or supermarket to look at different sea creatures. Take clipboards along to draw pictures and write lists of items seen.

● Purchase a fish and invite the children to touch and smell it. What do they think it feels like? Do they like the smell? Observe the scales and fins closely with a magnifying glass. Talk about the function of the fins.

⚠ **Note:** Make sure the children do not try to eat the fish and remind them to wash their hands thoroughly after handling it. Be aware of any allergies to fish.

jellyfish

Home Links

● Suggest that parents and carers take their children to a pet shop or aquarium to look at fish in tanks.

● Send home a simple biscuit recipe so that parents can make edible sea creature biscuits with their children.

Our Walk

Learning Intentions

- To use tools and equipment one-handed.

- To use a pencil and hold it effectively.

Our walk

Starting Points

- Take the children for a short walk around the locality. Point out buildings and features such as bridges, trees and fences. Talk about the traffic and the people that they see. Take photographs as you walk.

- On return to the classroom, ask the children to recall the walk and the things that they saw. Suggest making a drawing of the walk on a large piece of paper, encouraging the children to discuss what should be included in it. Keep the finished work and have the photographs developed, and use both in the display.

- Attach the photographs to a whiteboard. Invite the children to draw lines between each photograph with a board marker to plot the route taken.

Display

- Look again at the drawing of the walk made by the children (see 'Starting Points') and at the photographs taken. Talk about how to represent the things on the drawings and in the photographs (e.g. trees, cars, lampposts) using creative techniques and recycled materials.

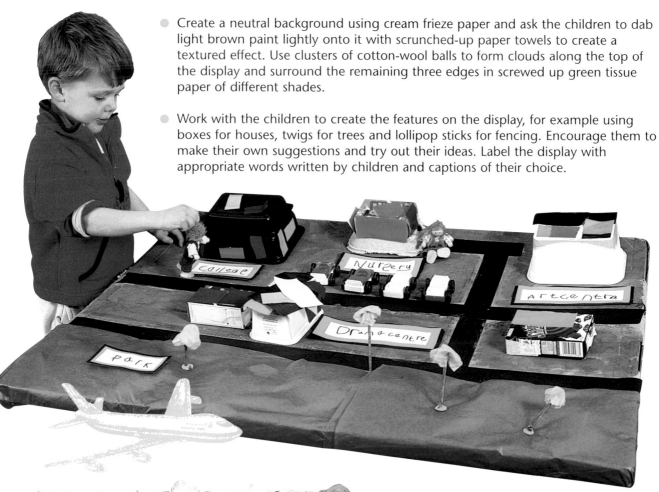

● Create a neutral background using cream frieze paper and ask the children to dab light brown paint lightly onto it with scrunched-up paper towels to create a textured effect. Use clusters of cotton-wool balls to form clouds along the top of the display and surround the remaining three edges in screwed up green tissue paper of different shades.

● Work with the children to create the features on the display, for example using boxes for houses, twigs for trees and lollipop sticks for fencing. Encourage them to make their own suggestions and try out their ideas. Label the display with appropriate words written by children and captions of their choice.

Free Play

● Create a 3D model of the walk using boxes and other recycled materials for the buildings and other features. Introduce small world people and vehicles and encourage the children to play freely with the resources available.

● Include road and rail layout mats alongside construction and small world equipment in a carpeted area so that children can play imaginatively using the experience of their walk to extend their ideas.

● Include clipboards and pencils alongside large construction equipment so that children can draw plans depicting what they are going to make with the equipment available.

Language and Literacy

- Draw a simple miniature version of the display and invite the children to move pencils along the paper to indicate the route of their journey from start to finish.

- Create miniature road signs on card for the display and models. Encourage the children to draw their own signs, looking at photographs and pictures for ideas.

- Set up role-play 'journey' opportunities by including large-scale maps, rucksacks and small suitcases in the role-play area. Join in with the children's play and make suggestions for imaginary journeys across the room.

Mathematics

- Look for numbers in the environment during the walk and then introduce these into the display or models, for example door and bus numbers, and speed limit signs.

- Use mathematical language related to position and order as you play with children with small world layouts, for example "Put trains on a track" and talk about which carriage is at the front and what colour the third carriage is, or talk about how the train travels under the bridge and over the level crossing.

- Invite children to take paintbrushes or rollers dipped in paint on journeys along lengths of wallpaper unrolled onto the floor to form road and rail tracks. Try creating contrasting straight and wavy lines.

Railtrack and road made with sponge rollers

straight

curved

Creative Work

- Use packing cases to create vehicles large enough for the children to sit inside and travel on imaginary journeys. Supply large decorators' brushes to paint them.

- Cover a table with a mixture of wallpaper paste and paint and invite the children to create tracks across the surface using their fingers or small plastic cars. Demonstrate how to wipe the surface with a paint roller and start again.

Our World

- Invite the children to create other layouts for small world play using papier-mâché on a strong board, for example a country scene or a dinosaur island.

- Show the children a large-scale map of the area and point out features they are familiar with. Display the map on the wall in the construction area.

- Set out large apparatus outside to form an obstacle course so that the children can make imaginary journeys up and down hills, under bridges and over rivers.

- As a group, take a journey by bus or train and note features on the way. On return to the classroom, make a class book about the experience using children's drawings, photographs and captions chosen and written by the children or scribed by adults.

Home Links

- Ask parents and carers to draw their children's attention to the route taken from home to the school setting. Suggest that they discuss the mode of travel and point out significant features.

- Invite parents and carers to accompany their children on a planned journey by bus or train.

Let's Post It!

Learning Intentions

- To use writing as a means of communicating.

- To recognise that print has meaning.

Starting Points

- Ask a child to dress up as a postal worker and talk with everyone about the mail delivered to their houses. Do they ever receive personal mail such as cards or parcels?

- Write a letter to the children and post it so that it is delivered to the school. When the letter arrives, discuss the contents, introducing the words 'envelope', 'stamp', 'postmark' and 'address'. Talk about people to whom the children might like to write letters.

- Write a letter together to the manager of the local sorting office asking if a postal worker could visit to talk to the children about collecting and delivering mail.

Display

- Back the display board with brightly-coloured paper and create a border from used stamps attached to strips of card. Encourage the children to arrange the stamps in patterns of different colours.

- Invite the children to help to create a montage by gluing handwritten letters, greetings cards, junk mail and postcards all over the surface of the backing paper. Attach cards by the back so that the writing inside can be seen.

- Name the different examples of mail as you work together and print out labels for the display. Point out handwritten and typed words and discuss the differences. Challenge the children to identify individual letters and words.

- Wrap a rectangular box in brown paper to form a parcel and tie string around it. Write a label 'Let's Post It!' in thick black letters and attach it to the display.

Free Play

- Create a role-play sorting office by forming a grid of shoeboxes. Arrange a row of boxes along the back of a long table, taped together securely, and then tape another two rows of boxes above them. Attach name labels to the boxes and encourage the children to sort a sack of pretend mail into the appropriate dockets. Stand a box at the side of the table for incoming mail and supply a rubber stamp to create postmarks.

- Use the same idea to create a storage system for the children's personal belongings. Stand this near the entrance to your setting so that children can store their things there ready to take home.

- Include balance scales in a role-play post office so that children can compare the weights of their home-made parcels.

Language and Literacy

- Set up a table under the display with resources for writing letters, greetings cards and postcards. Include a set of name cards so that children can write the names of their friends on letters, cards and envelopes. Stand a small postbox next to the table so that the letters can be posted.

- Invite the children to take turns to choose from a selection of postcards featuring images that they will find interesting, such as animals, children, unusual buildings or holiday resorts, and ask them to describe what they can see to the rest of the group.

- Play 'Envelope Snap', matching envelopes by the colour, or names of the recipients.

Mathematics

- Sort a pile of envelopes by size, shape or colour.

- Guess the contents of parcels by their shape. Introduce appropriate language such as 'bigger', 'smaller', 'cube', 'cuboid', 'cylinder' and 'sphere'.

- Ask the children to wrap up different-sized parcels, choosing appropriately-sized and shaped pieces of paper from a varied selection. Are any sizes more difficult to wrap than others? Why?

- Introduce coins into post office role-play so that children can pay for postage.

Creative Work

- Guess the contents of a parcel by the sound it makes when shaken. Ask the children to think of words to describe the sounds they hear.

- Invite the children to create their own stamps by printing designs on card, for example with cotton reels or small construction bricks.

- Look at a postal worker's uniform. What do they wear? What colours are there? What shapes are there?

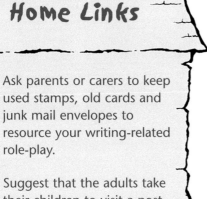

Our World

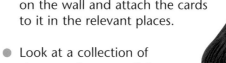

- Take a small group of children to a postbox to post letters that they have written. Discuss other street furniture on the way.

- Examine a selection of postcards of well-known features within the locality and then go for a walk to try to locate them.

- Explain the journey of a letter from when it is posted to when it is delivered. Invite children to send postcards whilst they are on holiday and look for the locations on a map of the world. Display the map on the wall and attach the cards to it in the relevant places.

- Look at a collection of stamps using magnifying glasses, focusing on the different pictures and patterns that can be seen.

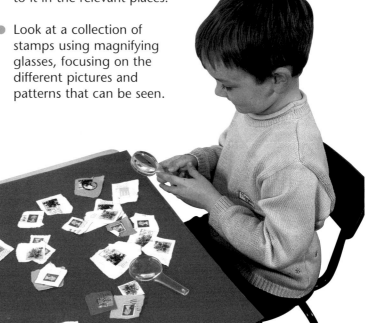

Home Links

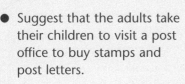

- Ask parents or carers to keep used stamps, old cards and junk mail envelopes to resource your writing-related role-play.

- Suggest that the adults take their children to visit a post office to buy stamps and post letters.

In the Jungle

Learning Intentions

- To draw and paint and to give meanings to marks.

- To express ideas through the written word.

Display

- Cut out a piece of green paper slightly larger than the display board and place onto a washable floor with lots of space around it. Invite the children to sponge-print lots of different shades of green all over the surface and leave the paper to dry before attaching it to the wall at child height.

Starting Points

- Visit the library with a small group of children and ask the librarian to help you find non-fiction books and stories about jungle animals. Borrow the books to take back to your setting. Look at the non-fiction books together and try to identify birds, reptiles, insects and animals that live in the jungle. Read the information and talk about the characters.

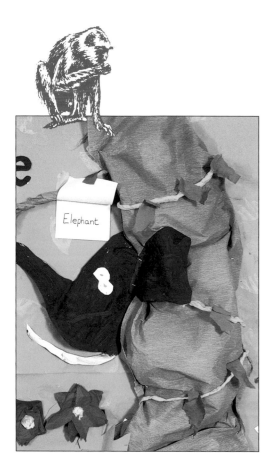

● Prompt the children to make different jungle creatures from collage materials and paint. Look at books to give an idea of features, colours, sizes and shapes.

● Create some large trees from newspaper. Roll the sheets of paper into tubes and then squeeze them to form an undulating surface. Staple the tubes loosely to the display to form tree trunks, then cover them with brown tissue paper. Push the jungle creatures behind the trees with small parts showing, such as an elephant's trunk or monkey's leg, to give the impression that they are hiding.

● Create the border by asking the children to twist strips of green tissue paper around lengths of rope at intervals to represent creepers. Pin the creepers around the edge of the display and hang some in front of it for added effect.

● Create some cards with the names of the hidden creatures written clearly on them. Hide the names by attaching a flap to the front of the card and secure a small piece of ribbon to the bottom so that the flap can be lifted up to reveal the word. Attach the cards to the display alongside the appropriate hidden creatures. Invite the children to guess the hidden creatures before lifting the flaps to check if they are correct.

Free Play

● Set up a table below the display with a model jungle using toy animals, grasses and cardboard trees.

● Make creatures for the jungle from Plasticine.

● Create a jungle role-play area by draping rope 'creepers' from the ceiling and setting up an obstacle course from large apparatus, such as a low climbing frame, tunnels, hoops and benches. Supervise the children as they play freely, emphasising that they should not pull on the creepers for safety reasons.

Language and Literacy

- Invite the children to make up their own jungle stories and dramatise them in your obstacle course role-play.

- Look at some lift-the-flap books. Suggest that the children make their own jungle books with lift-up flaps on each page and drawings of animals underneath. Try to link the text with the display by including pictures of the same creatures. Ask the children to write the words 'Who am I?' at the bottom of each page and then the name of the animal on top of the flap. They can copy the words from the display or use printed cards. Hang the home-made books along a string at the front of the display.

Mathematics

- Make a jungle counting frieze. Use collage materials to create different textures, for example shiny silk scraps for the skin of a snake, fur fabric for a monkey's coat and brightly-coloured crêpe paper for a parrot's feathers. Cut out numerals from textured paper and invite the children to run their fingers over the creatures and numerals as they count.

- Count the hidden creatures on the display together.

- Use the small world model creatures to sort, match and make comparisons.

Creative Work

- Create large picture/word cards of jungle creatures. In a large space, suggest that the children take it in turns to hold up a card whilst the others move like the animal depicted.

- Listen to different music and invent jungle movements, for example plodding to a slow beat like an elephant, flitting lightly around like birds and insects or jumping through the trees like monkeys.

Our World

- Look at a range of non-fiction books and models to compare the features of the jungle creatures.

- Look at a map of the world and talk about the location of jungles. Discuss what the climate might be like and decide together what the children might wear for a jungle trek.

- Create a model of a person travelling through the jungle using collage materials. Dress the model in appropriate clothing and display it with any objects needed for the journey, for example a water bottle and a camera. Make appropriate labels for clothing and additional items.

Home Links

- Suggest that parents or carers take their children to visit a zoo or safari park to see some of the creatures about which they have been learning.

Eating Out

Learning Intentions

- To explore different forms of writing, such as lists, recipes and menus.

- To use writing to record choices.

Starting Points

- Show the children examples of menus from cafés and restaurants and talk about their experiences of eating out.

- Visit a restaurant with the children and take photographs for later discussion.

Display

- Back a display board in brightly-coloured wallpaper and create a window from foil and card strips at the top. Hang two strips of a suitable fabric, such as gingham, at either side of the window to represent curtains. Decide upon a name for the café and write this in large letters on a strip of card and hang it in the window.

- Encourage the children to help to design posters depicting 'Special Offers' and 'Dish of the Day', and hang them on the display at either side of the window.

- Make a border from pictures of food painted by the children. Beneath the window, fasten a rectangle of fabric, matching the curtains if possible, to represent a tablecloth and 'Set the table' for two people by sticking plastic cutlery to the cloth.

- Create items of food from sponge pieces, paint them and glue them to two paper plates. Fasten the plates between the cutlery. Design menus with the children and staple these to the table and any spaces on the display.

- Invite the children to paint two customers and stick them to the display as if they were seated at the table.

- Ensure that there are lots of print examples on the display, such as prices, menus, posters and the name of the café.

Free Play

- Arrange two small tables below the display. Cover one in a cloth and set it for two. Stand menus in the centre, and ensure that there are two chairs and a box of hats available for 'customers'.

- Arrange a till, money, apron, notepad, pencil and receipt book for receiving orders and taking payment on the other table for café staff. Encourage the children to use the area as a small role-play café. Model appropriate behaviour by enacting the roles of both customer and staff. Demonstrate how to read the menu, take orders and give receipts.

- Include appropriate clothes and jewellery in the home area so that the children can dress up for a special celebratory meal at the restaurant.

Party Menu

Purple parsnips 3p

Popping peas 1p

Peanut pizza 20p

Prickly pears 10p

Parsley pie 8p

Language and Literacy

● Design different themed alphabet menus, or try to create a menu with one item for each letter of the alphabet, all items starting with the same letter or with rhyming items.

● Set up a role-play picnic trip, writing lists of what will be needed. Show the children how to tick off the items on their lists as they pack them to ensure that they have not left anything behind.

Mathematics

● Make placemats from card, laminate them and use them for one-to-one matching when setting the tables for the children's snacks and meals, or during role-play experiences.

● Play games involving matching cups, plates and cutlery by colour or size.

● Include money in café role-play and encourage the children to pay for items and receive change.

Creative Work

- Create an ice-cream stall with cardboard cones and lollipops. Encourage the children to make price labels and lists of choices for ice-cream flavours. Make cardboard ice-cream cones and fill them with cotton-wool ice-cream. Make paper lollies as well.

- Make artificial flowers from tissue and garden canes to decorate the tables of a role-play café.

- Create collage menus using pictures of meals cut from magazines.

Our World

- Take a small group of children to visit a café for a snack. Ask the proprietor if they may look at the area where food is prepared (arrange this in advance).

Home Links

- If possible, suggest that parents or carers provide opportunities for their children to experience eating out in cafés and restaurants that represent different cultures.

- Ask parents or carers to bring in examples of menus for the children to look at.

⚠ **Note:** Ensure that appropriate health and safety precautions are considered. Also remember to check for food allergies and dietary restrictions before allowing children to handle or taste different foods.

- Create step-by-step instructions for making a fruit milkshake on a series of cards using pictures and simple text. Invite the children to follow the cards in sequence to create drinks for snack time.

- Follow a simple recipe book or card to make snacks such as hot dogs or biscuits.

- Hold tasting sessions to sample food from different cultures, such as prawn crackers, pizzas or samosas.

- Discuss appropriate behaviour when eating out. Stress the importance of good manners and hygienic practices when handling food.

Let's Celebrate!

Learning Intentions

- To express ideas through drawing and making marks.

- To use writing to communicate feelings.

Starting Points

- Invite the children to bring in a favourite birthday present and talk to the others about why they like it. Alternatively, ask children to draw their favourite presents on a whiteboard.

- Discuss the children's memories of birthday celebrations. What did they enjoy most? What party games do they like playing?

- Sing *Happy Birthday* to a child or toy on the appropriate day.

Display

- Back a display board with brightly-coloured paper and add a contrasting border. Ask the children to make a large collage 'birthday' boy and girl to go in the middle of the display. What would appropriate party clothing be?

- Stuff some party gift bags with tissue paper, or wrap some boxes in birthday wrapping paper to create parcels, and attach these to the display. Give one gift to each of the birthday characters to hold.

- Surround the remaining space around the birthday characters with the cards, hats, party favours party invitations and napkins.

- Attach a big and bold 'Happy Birthday' banner across the top of the display. Decorate it with computer clip art images or ask the children to draw and colour some pictures.

- Blow up balloons and tie some thread to them. Tape these to the hand of one of the figures.

Free Play

- Provide party clothes for the children and toys, cards and wrapped parcels in the role-play area to encourage the children to set up imaginary parties.

- Leave a tea set, an artificial cake with candles and some birthday cards in a box outdoors to stimulate birthday party role-play.

⚠ **Note:** Remind the children that they should never play with matches and candles unless an adult is present.

- Set up a table under the display with resources for making birthday cards, such as felt-tip pens or crayons, glue sticks, a set of name cards, sequins and foil numbers. Encourage the children to explore the resources freely.

- Provide a tray of coloured shapes and numbers cut out from sticky paper. Have this available for the children to make their own birthday cards.

Language and Literacy

- Help the children to write birthday cards for friends or family members. Discuss a special message that they might like to write in the cards and scribe the children's word. Invite the children to write their names underneath.

- Plan a party for a toy or doll and encourage the children to write cards and send invitations to the rest of the toys in the role-play area.

Mathematics

- Sort a pile of children's birthday cards into different ages according to the numbers on the front.

- Make birthday cakes from modelling clay and push the appropriate number of candles into them. Talk about how many candles there will be if one more is added or taken away.

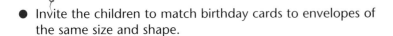

- Invite the children to match birthday cards to envelopes of the same size and shape.

- Use mathematical language as you make some small cakes for a birthday party together. Discuss the quantities required and weigh out the ingredients using appropriate vocabulary such as 'more', 'less' and 'full'. Count out spoons of flour and sugar as you transfer them from bag to scale. Once the cakes are baked, talk about how many you will need to put on a plate to ensure that each child has one. Count to check that there are sufficient.

Creative Work

- Invite the children to paint pictures of their birthday gifts and arrange them in a book entitled 'Our Favourite Presents'.

- Play the 'Our Favourite Presents' game. Create a parcel from a lidded box covered with birthday wrapping paper. Invite each child to choose a birthday present from a toy catalogue, cut it out, glue it to a square of card, put the card in the box and close the lid. Pass the parcel containing the cards around to music. When the music stops, ask the child holding the parcel to take out a card and hold it up. Whoever chooses the present on the card then talks about their choice and keeps the card. The game continues until the box is empty.

- Create an artificial cake from a box covered in plaster of Paris to represent icing. Attach candleholders before the plaster dries. Push the appropriate number of candles into the holders when a child celebrates a birthday so that they can be lit and blown out as the rest of the class sings *Happy Birthday*.

⚠ **Note:** Supervise the children closely when near candle flames.

- Play party games involving dancing to music, such as 'Musical Statues', 'Musical Bumps' and 'Pass the Parcel'.

Our World

- Encourage the children to create cards for different cultural and religious festivals, such as Easter and Chinese New Year. Invite parents from different cultures to donate examples of such cards, and to talk about the traditions associated with the celebration.

- Talk about the significance of lighting candles during festivals of light, such as Diwali, Hanukkah and Christmas.

- Follow a recipe for simple sponge cup cakes and decorate them with icing. Talk about the changes observed as the ingredients are mixed and then heated. Talk about the everyday uses of technology such as ovens, microwaves, fridges or mixers.

Home Links

- Ask parents or carers to donate their children's old birthday cards for the activities. Try to collect a wide range of ages.

- Invite parents and grandparents to talk to the children about their memories of birthday celebrations when they were children.

Juicy Favourites

Learning Intentions

- To write their own names as a means of identification.

- To begin to name and sound some of the letters in their name.

Starting Points

- Visit a fruit stall or supermarket with a small group of children and name the fruits for sale. Buy some samples to taste.

⚠ **Note:** Ensure that appropriate health and safety precautions are considered. Also remember to check for food allergies and dietary restrictions before letting children handle or taste different foods.

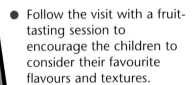

- Follow the visit with a fruit-tasting session to encourage the children to consider their favourite flavours and textures.

Display

- Back a low-level display board in yellow paper and ask the children to surround it with paper oranges and lemons as a border.

- Create a graph of favourite fruits by drawing a grid with numbers from 1 to 10 in the squares on the left-hand side and outlines of the fruits tasted in the squares along the top. Prepare some paper outlines of the fruits to be tasted. Ask the children to taste the fruits and then write their name on a sticky label and attach it to an outline of their chosen fruit. Help them to stick this into a square on the correct column of the graph. Mount the graph in the centre of the display.

- Invite the children to paint pictures of their favourite fruits and mount these on orange paper to add to the display.

- Create a title for the display in clear lettering, for example 'Juicy Favourites'.

Free Play

- Include plastic fruit in the home corner to encourage conversation about preferences and taste.

- Leave a bowl of fruit in the creative area to encourage the children to try to paint and draw the different types.

- Set up a role-play fruit stall using papier-mâché or plastic fruit. Encourage the children to count, sort, weigh and match their purchases and to pay for them and receive change. Also include writing materials for receipts and shopping lots.

Language and Literacy

- Play fruit 'I Spy' with real or plastic fruit.

- Set up a table at either side of the display. Arrange paper plates, a set of name cards, some writing tools and a basket of plastic fruit on one table. Invite the children to write their names on paper plates, using name cards to help, if necessary, and then to each choose a piece of plastic fruit representing their favourite from the basket to put on a paper plate. Ask them to take the plates carefully to the other table to display.

Mathematics

- Use the plates of fruit to introduce simple problems, for example asking the children which fruit is the most popular and which is the least, and how they know this. Encourage them to count and use the words 'more' and 'less'.

- Arrange the plates on the floor in rows of similar fruits to form a 3D graph.

- Look carefully at the pictograph on the display. Ask questions such as "How many more people liked bananas than oranges?" "Which fruit was liked by the most children?" "Which fruit was liked by the fewest children?"

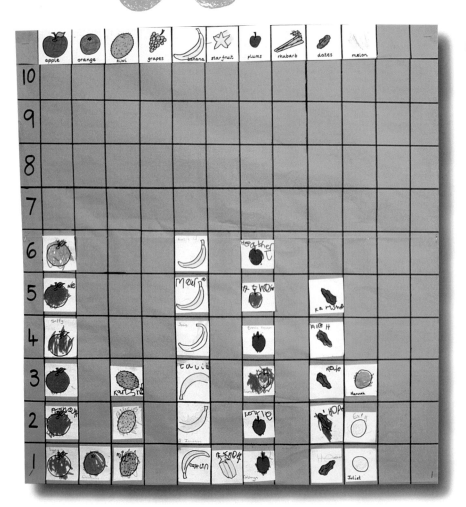

Creative Work

- Create a picture of a fruit tree, making the trunk and branches from scrunched-up newspaper painted brown, leaves from curled green tissue and fruits by painting a fruit of the children's choice.

- Paint hand-print trees. Cover the palm, fingers and thumb of one hand with brown paint and then press it down on a sheet of paper to form a tree-shaped print. Explore colours to create fruit for the tree using thumb and fingerprints.

Hand print trees

Thumb print fruit

Grass printed with the side of the finger

Our World

- Explore the shape, texture and taste of unusual and exotic fruits from around the world, such as lychees and pawpaws. Look on a map to locate their country of origin.

- Show the children tinned, fresh, frozen and dried versions of a fruit such as apricots or apples. Talk about how fruit can be preserved. Taste the samples and make comparisons.

- Make a collection of fruit (fresh, dried and tinned) and products that contain fruit and display it on a table with labels.

- Try to identify different fruits using the sense of smell alone.

Home Links

- Invite a parent or carer who is a keen gardener to come and talk about growing fruit, and to bring in some homegrown produce.

- Ask the adults to stew some fruit so that children can compare cooked and fresh produce.

All these things have fruit in them.

Can you name the fruit in the basket?

Orange Plums Kiwi Apple Dates

Feel the Letters

Learning Intentions

- To name and sound the letters of the alphabet.

- To recognise the initial letter sounds of words.

Starting Points

- Play 'I Spy' and talk about the initial letter sounds of words.

- Ask the children what sound their names begin with.

- Look at alphabet books and charts. Identify the objects on the pictures and talk about their initial sounds.

- Make a chart with a picture for each letter of the alphabet. Talk about the initial letter sounds of each picture and invite a child to attach the appropriate letter (using Velcro dots or sticky tack).

Display

- Back a display board at child height with brightly-coloured paper and make the border from cut-out paper, sponge or plastic letters.

- Choose some small objects such as a toy car, an orange, a ribbon and a plastic snake, and cut out large lower-case letters from card depicting the object's initial letters. Cover the letters with collage materials of different textures such as sand, wood shavings, seeds, sponge pieces, velvet scraps and textured wallpaper. Stick the letters to the display and invite the children to run their fingers over the outlines. Put a caption at the top of the display, for example, 'Come and Touch'.

- Make a collection of objects with the same initial letter sound. Put the small objects in individual trays and attach the appropriate initial letter to each tray. Suspend the trays from the top of the display using lengths of thin string. Encourage the children to make the link between the large display letters, the small tray letters and the initial letters of each object.

Free Play

- Include plastic letters on a table with lumps of modelling clay to encourage children to press letters from the clay.

- Float sponge or plastic letters in the water tray and supply fishing nets so that the children can fish for the letters in their names.

- Hide plastic or wooden letters in dry sand and supply small spades so that children can dig them up, saying the sounds and letter names as each is found.

Language and Literacy

- Leave a box of letters on the table under the display. Encourage the children to feel the letters on the wall and try to match the cards on the table to the objects, or to the wall letters.

- Set up another table near the display with paper, word cards and matching objects, and mark-making equipment, so that children can draw the objects and copy or write the words beside them. Attach a small notice board to the wall behind the table, if possible, for children to display their work themselves.

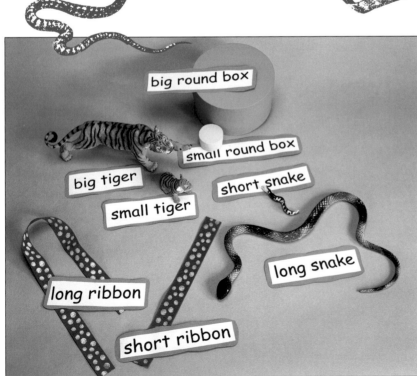

Mathematics

- Hide the objects from the table in different positions around the room. Invite the children to choose a letter card from the box and then try to find something beginning with that letter. Give clues related to position, such as 'under' the chair or 'behind' the doll's house.

- Play a game involving matching pairs of similar objects but ensure that they have different colours or sizes, for example a small and large orange or a long and short ribbon. Invite the children to find two similar objects and then ask appropriate questions, such as "Which is the longest snake?" or "Which is the biggest lorry?"

Creative Work

- Create letters from thick card and put them in a bag. Invite the children to take turns to put a hand in the bag and guess the letter they are holding, using only the sense of touch. Ask them to pull the letter out of the bag to see if they have guessed correctly.

- Sew letters onto open-weave fabric squares using thick wool. Glue the squares onto white sheeting to create a letter patchwork.

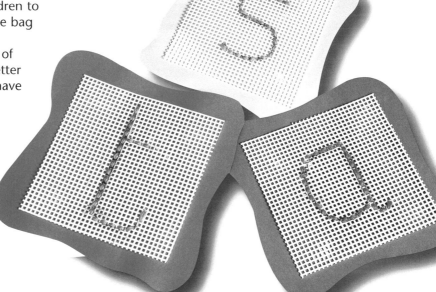

Our World

- Make letters from different materials such as wood, clay, card, foil and sponge. Experiment to see whether the letters will float or sink.

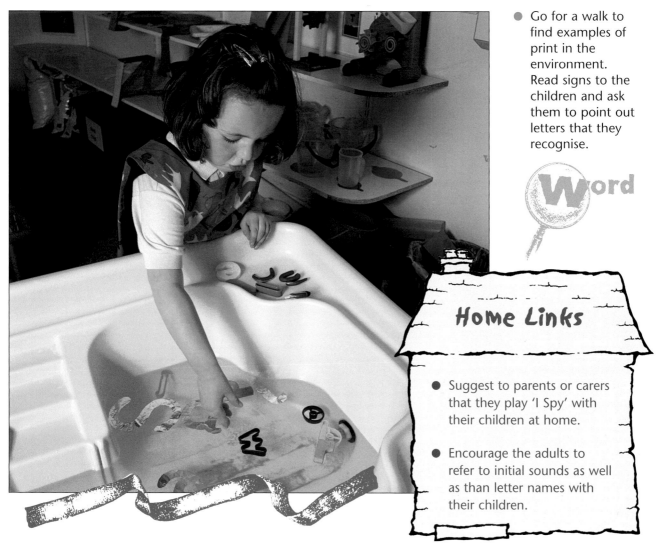

- Go for a walk to find examples of print in the environment. Read signs to the children and ask them to point out letters that they recognise.

Home Links

- Suggest to parents or carers that they play 'I Spy' with their children at home.

- Encourage the adults to refer to initial sounds as well as than letter names with their children.

Who Is This?

Learning Intentions

● To recognise and write their names.

● To know that print in the form of labels and captions carries meaning.

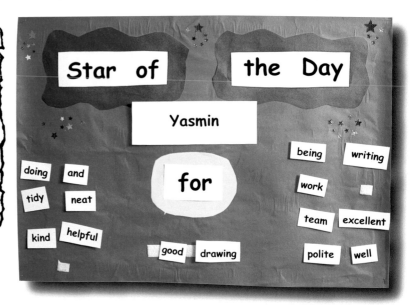

Starting Points

● Ask the class to bring in some photographs of themselves from home. Pass around the photographs and talk about differences in appearance, such as eye, hair and skin colour. Encourage respect for differences.

● Make a 'Star of the Day' chart to celebrate individual children's achievements.

Display

- Back the display board in brightly-coloured paper. Invite the children to create a border by drawing happy faces on coloured circles of card and sticking them around the edge of the display.

- Mount the children's photographs on squares of card. Tape them to the top edge of the squares, above the photographs. Attach small pieces of ribbon to the bottom of the flaps so that they can be lifted to reveal the photograph underneath.

- Help the children to type their names on a computer, print them and then cut them so that they fit on the front of the flap. Glue the names in place and attach the cards to the display. Create a display title in bold letters, such as 'Who is this?'.

- Invite the children to find their names on the display and suggest that they lift the flap to check that they are correct.

Free Play

- Set up a table with a safety mirror and some mark-making tools and materials so that the children can draw their faces, paying attention to detail.

- Invite the children to play freely on outdoor apparatus. Make a large scrapbook page showing the equipment in the outdoor area. Suggest that the children write their names or make their mark alongside their favourite piece of apparatus in the book. Look at the book later, to decide the most popular piece of apparatus.

49

Language and Literacy

- Encourage the children to look at a selection of lift-the-flap books and suggest that they make their own books with flaps to reveal their favourite things, such as toys or foods.

- Make some simple three-letter word cards and separate pictures. Encourage the children to match the correct word to the picture by saying the initial letter sound (and blending the others) to make the word.

- Create a role-play photo booth from a large packaging case. Encourage the children to draw passport-size self-portraits, and to write appropriate captions and signs, to display on the outside.

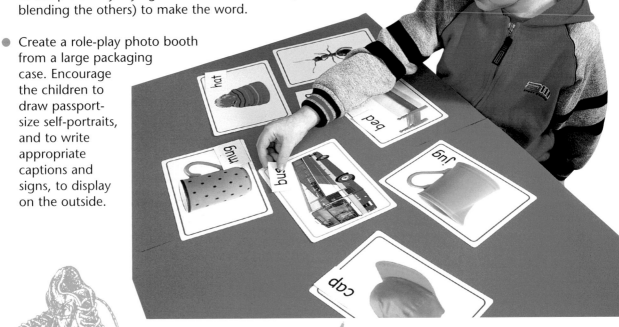

Mathematics

- Play a 'Recognise and Check' game. Set out a row of boxes with numbers on the lids and the corresponding number of small objects inside. Ask the children to take turns to turn over a number card from a pile, identify it and match it with a number on one of the boxes before opening the box and counting the objects inside to check.

- Create a set of shoebox garages with lift-up doors. Number some small plastic cars and cut out paper silhouettes of them in matching colours. Stick one of the coloured silhouettes on the floor of each garage and write the car number on the door. Invite the children to drive the cars into the correct garages by matching their numbers, colours and shapes.

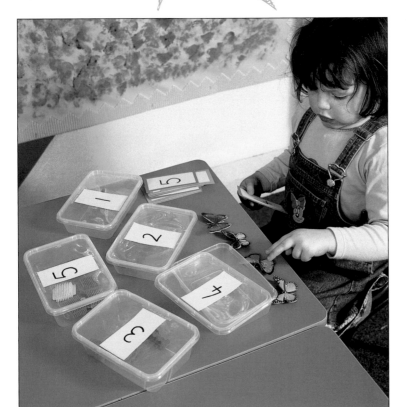

Creative Work

- Make 3D clay name plaques using flat tiles of clay as a base. Invite the children to form the letters of their name from clay and attach them to a tile with slip. When the plaque has dried, apply PVA glue as a varnish and sprinkle on glitter and seeds to give an interesting texture.

- Invite the children to create montages of their favourite things made by cutting pictures from magazines and catalogues. Use them to form the covers of 'All About Me' books.

- Paint self-portraits and make paper-plate face portraits using collage materials. Display these with a photograph of each child.

Our World

- Invite the children to make a book about themselves, suggesting their own captions to be scribed by an adult for them to copy.

- Design name pendants from a variety of materials and suspend from a loop of ribbon.

- Create a changeable sign saying 'Today's little helper' and invite the chosen child to suggest ways of looking after the indoor and outdoor environment, for example, tidying up or picking up litter.

Home Links

- Invite parents or carers to supply photographs of their children for the display.

- Set up the display in the entrance hall so that the adults can encourage their children to read their names.

Budding Authors

Starting Points

- Read stories by well-known children's authors and decide as a group which ones you prefer.

- Choose a favourite author and read several of his or her books. Talk about the characters. Does the same character appear in more than one book? Do the children have a favourite character? Can they say why they like this character?

Our favourite author is Ian Whybrow

We wrote a letter to Ian Whybrow and he sent us photographs of himself and Harry to hang on our wall.

We made books about Harry

Harry and the Robots

Harry and the Dinosaurs say 'Raahh!'

Harry and the Bucketful of Dinosaurs

Adrian Reynolds is the illustrator
He draws pictures of Harry

Our favourite character is Harry

We painted pictures of Harry

Display

- Choose a display board in or close to the story corner and back it in brightly-coloured paper. Display the children's home-made books (see 'Language and Literacy') all around the edge of the display to form a border.

- Print out captions stating who is the children's favourite author and character and attach these to the display.

- Surround the captions with copies of the books and the children's paintings and drawings of their favourite character.

- As a group, write a letter to the author to say why the story was enjoyed so much, who the favourite character was and why.

Free Play

- Encourage the children to re-enact their favourite stories using a selection of small world equipment and appropriate props, for example small plastic goats, strips of wood and small bricks to re-enact the *Three Billy Goats Gruff* story.

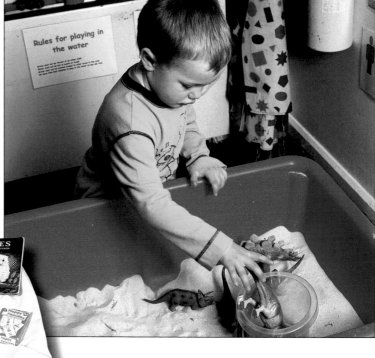

- Provide the children with resources linked to stories read, for example a selection of plastic dinosaurs and a large bucket balance to explore after reading *Harry and the Bucketful of Dinosaurs* by Ian Whybrow (Gullane Children's Books, 2002).

- Create story sacks of the children's favourite stories to stimulate dramatic play.

Language and Literacy

- Set up a table under the display with a tape recorder and tapes of favourite stories pre-recorded by staff members for children to listen to by themselves. Include mark-making equipment so that the children can draw and write their own versions of the stories.

- Record the children's made-up stories as they tell them, either on a tape or flip chart. Encourage them to make their own books based on these stories. Provide rectangles of paper and ask the children to fold them down the centre to create small books. Talk about their stories and ask them to think of titles. Write the title for them and add captions to their drawings.

- Ask the children to draw pictures of their stories and make them into sets of picture cards so that they can be arranged in sequence.

- Create a role-play library from which the children can pretend to borrow books.

Mathematics

- Make up games associated with favourite stories. For example, create a shape-matching game based on the robots in the story *Harry and the Robots* by Ian Whybrow (Gullane Children's Books, 2001). In this game, the children to find shapes to put on a robot outline to match the shapes on a robot made from coloured card copied from the book.

- Draw children's attention to page numbering in books and then ask them to write numbers in the correct order on the pages of their home-made books.

- Show the children a book index and talk about how looking for page numbers helps them to find what they are looking for. Invite them to peg card or plastic numbers in order on a washing line.

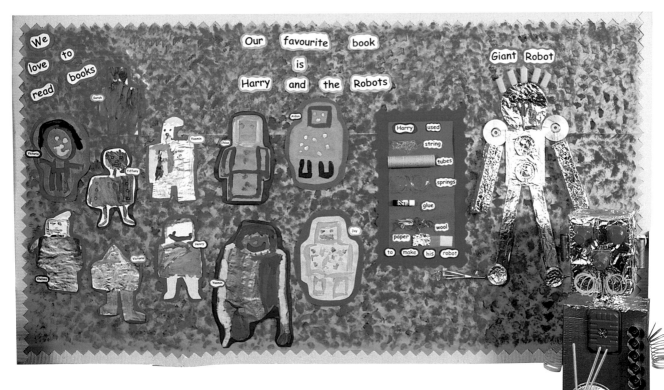

Creative Work

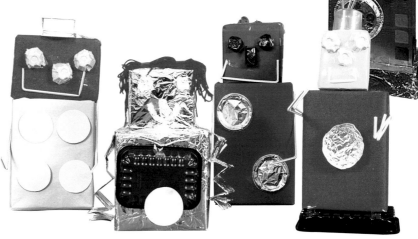

- Create a display about the children's favourite book alongside the favourite author display. Make 3D models of the storybook characters from recycled materials and stand these alongside the display. Paint pictures of favourite characters and attach these to the display.

Home Links

- Choose a favourite toy from the home corner, such as a teddy, and invite the children to take turns to take the teddy home for the weekend. Supply the toy with a diary and ask the children's families to help them to write about the toy's adventures in the diary.

Our World

- Plan story-related activities in different play areas, for example filling and emptying buckets and playing with plastic dinosaurs in the water tray after reading *Harry and the Bucketful of Dinosaurs* (published by Gullane).

- Examine how books with unusual designs are made, for example pop-up and lift-the-flap books. Explore 'feely', 'noisy' or perfumed books designed to stimulate the senses.

- Look to see whether the children's favourite author has a website and print out appropriate pictures and information to add to the display. Talk to the children about using a computer to find information.

What's Inside?

Learning Intentions

● To understand what is meant by 'word'.

● To use their phonic knowledge to read and write simple regular words.

Starting Points

● Look for some three-lettered words in books and count the letters. Ask the children to identify the first, last and middle letters. Try to sound them out together and blend them to make the word.

Display

● Back a display board at child height in yellow paper and create a border from letters printed randomly around the edge. Print an appropriate caption for the display, for example 'What's Inside?' or 'Come and Read'.

● Collect a selection of small objects with a simple spelling of consonant, vowel, consonant, such as a bed from a doll's house or a plastic pig. Print out two sets of the words representing the objects, one in small and one in large lower-case letters. Cut the words into rectangles. Mount the large words on red paper and attach them to the display.

Collect some small boxes with lids and glue a matching word from the display to the front of each one. Put the corresponding object in the box and close the lid. Arrange the boxes on a table under the display and tape a length of thin string with a large wooden bead threaded through it to the lid of each one. Join each string to the correct word on the display so that the children can move the bead from word to object and back again along the string.

Free Play

Leave a set of word cards, some small boxes and some objects on a table so that the children can play their own games. For example, they could hide the objects in boxes and put the appropriate word card alongside for other children to read to identify the contents of each box.

Encourage the children to attempt their own writing in the graphics area.

Language and Literacy

- Invite the children to choose one of the words on the display and to point to a matching word on one of the boxes below.

- Ask the children to try to read the words on the display and the boxes and to check if they are correct by opening the appropriate boxes.

- Provide paper, writing equipment and a matching set of word cards on a table alongside the display so that the children can attempt to write the words or draw pictures if they wish.

- Make a simple three-letter picture/word 'flap' book and invite the children to read the words before lifting the flap to reveal the picture underneath.

Mathematics

- Print out some words of different lengths and invite the children to count the letters. Decide which is the longest and shortest word and sort the words into groups according to the number of letters.

- Print out some positional words on cards, such as 'under', 'beside', 'on' or 'behind', and turn them upside down. Put a doll on a chair and then invite individual children to choose a card and put the doll in the position indicated on the card in relation to the chair.

Creative Work

- Invite the children to choose one of the cards used in the display, read the word and then paint a picture of the object.

- Pick three of the cards at random, such as 'hat', 'bed' and 'hen', and then make up and act out a story together involving the three objects.

- Make three-letter words from different textures. Encourage the children to feel the letters and then match them to a picture or object.

Our World

- Design a magic object box. Paint the inside of a shoebox black and then cut a small hole in the lid and the side. Create a flap over the hole in the lid so that it can be covered. Invite the children to stick stars around the inside of the box and place a three-letter object (such as a toy pig) to the bottom. Put the lid on the box and close the flap.

Home Links

- Set up the display near the entrance to your setting and invite parents to help their children to read the words on the display and check them by looking at the contents of the boxes.

- Invite the children to look through the hole in the side of the box using a torch and give clues as to what they can see. For example, "It begins with P". The other children try to guess what the object is.

What Can I Do?

Learning Intentions

- To use drawing, painting and writing to pass on information to others.

- To write simple words and attempt to write more complex words.

Starting Points

- Take the children outdoors and ask them to try different body movements, such as jumping, hopping, balancing on one leg and running. Talk about what they can do and invite them to suggest movements of their own for others to try to copy. Take photographs of the different movements.

- Play 'Follow My Leader' with an adult as leader, introducing a range of body movements to raise the children's awareness of the physical actions that they are capable of.

Display

- Back a display board in brightly-coloured paper and create a border by attaching ropes and beanbags around the edge. Print out an appropriate caption in large letters, such as 'What Can I Do?', and fasten this near the top of the display.

- Look at the children's drawings and paintings of their actions (see 'Creative Work') and invite them to suggest suitable captions. Scribe the children's chosen words on paper and suggest that they try to copy them. Glue the captions to the bottom of the picture and mount the finished pictures on coloured paper contrasting with the display backing paper.

- Mount the photographs taken of the children's actions (see 'Starting Points' and 'Our World') on the same coloured paper as the pictures. Arrange the mounted pictures and photographs on or near the display.

Free Play

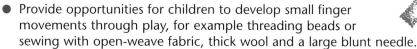

- Leave containers of small apparatus outdoors so that children can explore them freely.

- Provide opportunities for children to develop small finger movements through play, for example threading beads or sewing with open-weave fabric, thick wool and a large blunt needle.

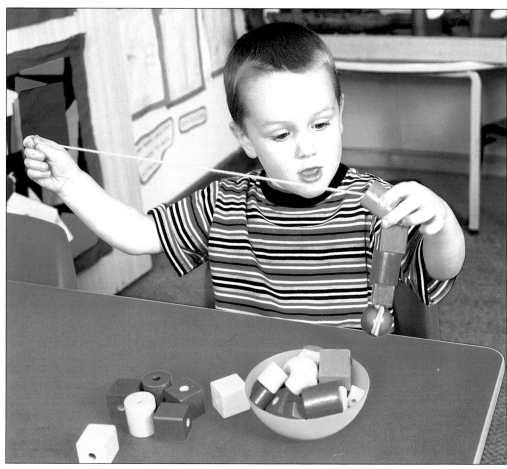

Language and Literacy

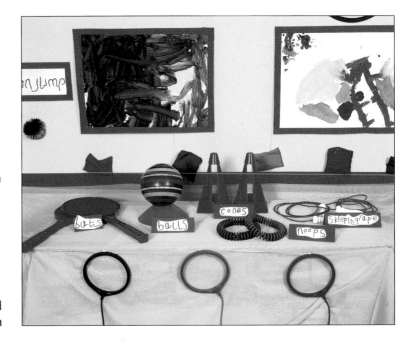

- Make 'What Can I Do?' books for each child using drawings, photographs and captions.

- Supply the children with thick chalk and invite them to draw long lines on the ground outdoors. Ask them to try to move along the lines in different ways, for example, on all fours, hopping or tiptoeing.

- Set up a table under the display with items related to physical activities, such as a beanbag, skipping rope and small hoop. Make labels for each item with the children.

- Set up a table near the display with an album containing photographs of children using the apparatus, as well as jumping, running, skipping and hopping. Supply lots of paper, crayons and felt-tip pens to stimulate discussion and mark-making.

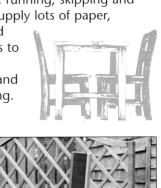

Mathematics

- Encourage the children to count as they hop and jump, or climb up the steps of a slide.

- Measure the distance in strides that the children can roll or throw a ball.

- Challenge the children to build high towers and then count the number of bricks used. Make comparisons between the numbers of bricks in each tower.

Creative Work

- Sing *Here We Go Round the Mulberry Bush* and include lots of physical actions, such as hopping, running, jumping, kneeling and stretching.

- Ask the children to stand in front of a mirror so that they can watch themselves moving in different ways. Have an easel nearby to encourage them to paint what they have observed.

- Supply crayons and large sheets of paper outdoors so that the children can draw pictures of their own movements and the movements of others on a large scale.

Our World

- Invite the children to explore a range of small apparatus, such as balls, beanbags, hoops and quoits, and take photographs of them as they do so.

- Have fun balancing beanbags on different parts of the body. Talk about the meaning of the word 'balance' and play freely with balance scales in a dry sand tray.

- Show the children examples of the special clothing needed for sports such as swimming, skiing and football. Talk about why such clothing is essential. Look at a catalogue displaying items of sports equipment and talk about how they are used.

- Ask some older children, or staff members, to demonstrate to the children how they can skip with a skipping rope both individually and in a group.

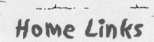

Home Links

- Invite parents or carers to a fun sports day with activities designed to challenge the children without being too competitive; for example, throwing wet sponges at paper-plate faces hanging along a washing line.

- Invite parents or family members to talk to the children about sports they take part in and to show them some of the clothing and equipment they use.

Resourcing the Writing Area

There are many useful everyday resources to enable children to extend their mark-making skills. The following lists are for guidance and inspiration only, and are by no means comprehensive.

Mark-making Tools

- Pencils of different thicknesses, crayons, felt-tip pens, biros, chalk, candles

Mark-making Materials

- Paper, card, tissue, wallpaper, lining paper, greaseproof paper and cardboard of different colours, shapes, sizes and thicknesses

- Notepads, jotters, ready-made small books, diaries, appointment books, telephone pads, envelopes

- Fabric scraps

- Junk mail, calendars, forms

Additional Resources to Stimulate Writing

- Set of name cards

- Clipboards

- Alphabet posters and friezes, alphabet books, writing in a range of languages and scripts

- Computer and computer programs

- Cookery books and recipe cards, mail order catalogues and seed catalogues, magazines, telephone directories, maps

- Birthday and greetings cards, postcards

- Folders and files

- Whiteboard, notice board

- Message boxes or pockets, storage trays for children's work

- Telephone, calculator

- Scissors (both left- and right-handed)

- Joining materials such as glue sticks, sticky tape, stapler, paper clips, stickers

- Hole punch, date stamp

For those who have a limited amount of space, consider using a trolley, toolbox, large storage box or small set of office trays to store equipment and bring this out for each session. Store writing tools in labelled plastic containers. Trolleys provide ideal opportunities for outdoor mark-making.